PAPA'S MECHANICAL FISH

Candace Fleming

Pictures by Boris Kulikov

Margaret Ferguson Books
Farrar Straus Giroux
New York

Farrar Straus Giroux Books for Young Readers
175 Fifth Avenue, New York 10010

Text copyright © 2013 by Candace Fleming
Pictures copyright © 2013 by Boris Kulikov
All rights reserved
Color separations by Bright Arts (H.K.) Ltd.
Printed in China by South China Printing Co. Ltd.,
Dongguan City, Guangdong Province
Designed by Jay Colvin
First edition, 2013
1 3 5 7 9 10 8 6 4 2

mackids.com

Library of Congress Cataloging-in-Publication Data
Fleming, Candace.
    Papa's mechanical fish / Candace Fleming ; pictures by Boris Kulikov. — 1st ed.
        p.   cm.
    Summary: In the summer of 1851, with encouragement and ideas provided by his family, an inventor
builds a working submarine and takes his family for a ride. Includes notes about Lodner Phillips,
the real inventor on whom the story is based.
    ISBN 978-0-374-39908-5 (hardcover)
    [1. Inventors—Fiction.   2. Family life—Fiction.   3. Submarines (Ships)—Fiction.   4. Phillips,
L. D. (Lodner Darvontis), 1825–1869—Fiction.]   I. Kulikov, Boris, 1966–   ill.   II. Title.

PZ7.F59936Pap 2013
[E]—dc23
                                                                                            2012029659

For Charlene and Carole—a hometown tale for my sisters extraordinaire. Wanna go to the beach, girls?
—C.F.

To Max, Andre, and Kate
—B.K.

This is my papa.
   And this is his backyard workshop, where he spends his days
thinking . . .
            tinkering . . .
                  and inventing things.
Hear that?
Clink! Clankety-bang! Thump-whirrrr!
That's the sound of Papa at work.
Clink! Clankety-bang! Thump-whirrrr!

Sometimes Papa tries inventing helpful things, like collapsible coat hangers that are easy to store.

Sometimes he tries inventing unusual things, like edible socks.

And sometimes he tries inventing playful things that just—only just—don't work, like steam-powered roller skates. (He forgot to put the brakes on.)

But not once has Papa invented anything that works perfectly.
"I will someday," Papa tells me. "All I need is a fantastic idea."
But fantastic ideas are not easy to come by.

So Papa twiddles his tools and pulls his hair. He racks his brain, sighs, and stares until one day he throws down his screwdriver. "Enough thinking!" he cries. "Who wants to go fishing?"

"I do!" I holler.

"Me, too," says my brother, Cyril.

"Don't forget me," adds our sister Mary.

"My daa-daa!" squeals the baby, Wilhelmina.

"Woof!" barks our bulldog, Rex.

"I'm so glad I brought along these poles," says Mama.

We all troop out to the lighthouse pier and drop our lines into Lake Michigan.

Plop! Plop! Plop! Plop! Plop!

"Papa," I say as we wait for a bite, "have you ever wondered what it's like to be a fish?"

"A fish?" he mutters. "A fish?"

"Uh-oh," squeals the baby.

Papa's pole clatters to the pier. He leaps to his feet. He whirls me around. "Virena, you're brilliant," he whoops.

Then he is gone, racing back over the sand dunes to his workshop.

Clink! Clankety-bang! Thump-whirrrr!

"Ta-da!" cries Papa a few weeks later. He opens his workshop doors to reveal . . .

"What is it?" I ask.

"It's an underwater vessel," he explains. "A mechanical fish. I will dive like a salmon. I will glide like a trout."

Papa's mechanical fish is so small he barely fits inside. It has a tube sticking out the top so he can breathe. It has a pole sticking out the bottom so he can push himself along the lake floor.

"I call it the *Whitefish*," he says.

But will it work?

We keep our fingers crossed.
"Goodbye, Papa." We wave.
"Farewell, family." He waves back.
Then the *Whitefish* is launched.
Sploosh!
But . . .

Glub-glub-glub!
Papa swims back to the pier.
"It almost worked," he says.

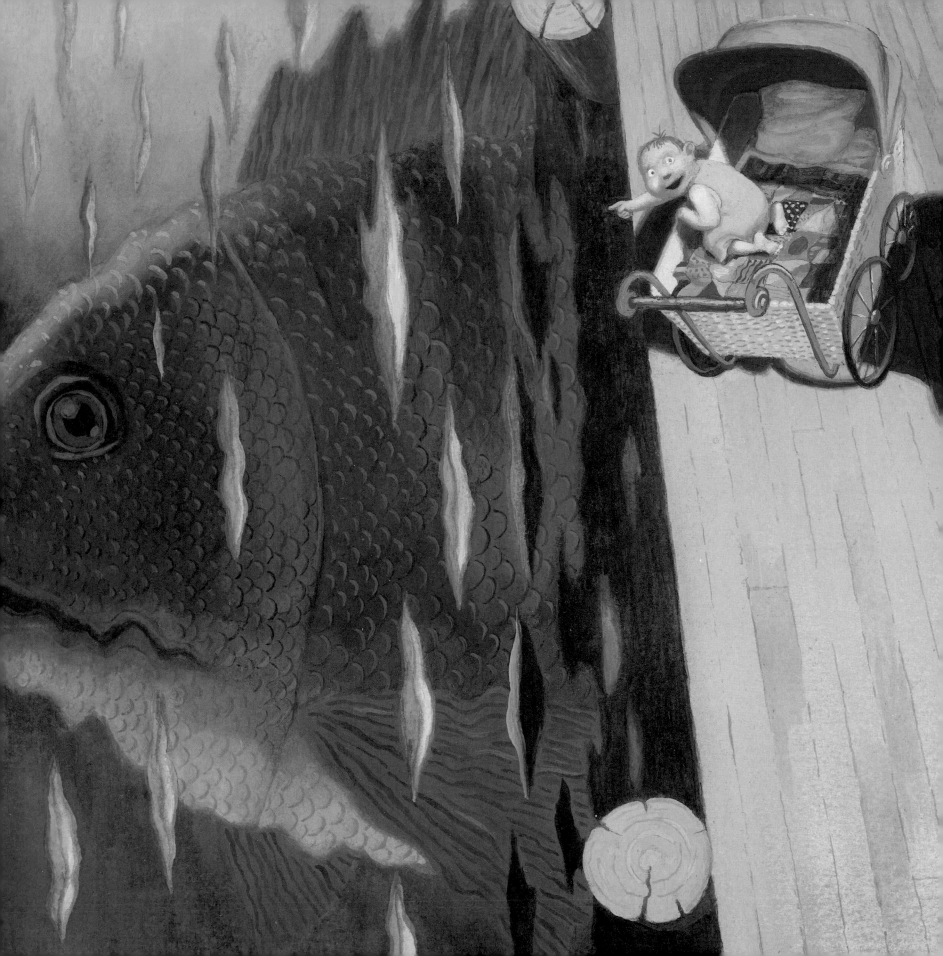

"Almost," I agree. I think for a minute, then ask, "Papa, how do fish move through the water?"

"With their tails?" says Cyril.

"With their fins?" adds Mary.

"Fishy go!" squeals the baby.

"Woof!" barks Rex.

"I'm so glad I brought along this towel," says Mama. She wraps it around Papa's shoulders.

But he is too deep in thought to notice.

And . . .

A — fin
B — propeller
C — second seat

Clink! Clankety-bang! Thump-whirrrr!
"Behold the *Whitefish II*."

It is big enough for two people to sit in. It has a wooden fin on top and a wooden propeller in back. Papa pedals it like a bicycle to make it go.

"Goodbye, Papa." We wave.

"Farewell, family." He waves back.

Then the *Whitefish II* is launched.

Sploosh!

It dives below the surface.

Swoosh!

But . . .

Crack–drip–splinter–rip!
Papa bobs to the surface.
"It almost worked," he hollers to us.

"Almost," I holler back. I think again, then ask, "Papa, how do fish stay dry?"

"With special skin?" asks Cyril.

"With scales?" adds Mary.

"No pee-pee!" squeals the baby.

"Woof!" barks Rex.

"I'm so glad I brought along this life preserver," says Mama. She tosses it to Papa.

But he is too deep in thought to notice.

And . . .

Within the illustration:

Whitefish 3.

D

C
B

A

A – extra seats
B – power
steering wheel
lowers
ver cover

Clink! Clankety-bang! Thump-whirrrr!
"Behold the *Whitefish III*."

It is big enough for three people to sit in. It has a plunger to make it go up and down. It has a steering wheel to make it go left and right. It has levers instead of pedals. And it is covered in waterproof copper.

"Goodbye, Papa." We wave.

"Farewell, family." He waves back.

Then the *Whitefish III* is launched.

Sploosh!

It dives.

Swoosh!

It chugs beneath the waves.

Clacketa-clacketa-clacketa!

But . . .

Cruuump!
Papa clings to a buoy.
"It almost worked," he says minutes later as we pull him into the rowboat.

"Almost," I say. I think some more, then ask, "Papa, how do fish know where they're going?"

"Can they see underwater?" says Cyril.

"Do they have good eyes?" adds Mary.

"Peekaboo!" squeals the baby.

"Woof!" barks Rex.

"I'm so glad I brought along these oars," says Mama. She rows toward shore.

But Papa is too deep in thought to notice.

Now he barricades himself in his workshop.

Clink! Clankety-bang! Thump-whirrrr!

He does not come out.

Thunk-clunk-whack!

We cannot go in.

Tap-tap!

He even covers the windows so we can't peek.

Zaaaaaap!

"What's the big secret?" I ask.

"Wait and see," Papa says. "Just wait and see."

Clink! Clankety-bang! Thump-whirrrr!

At last, he flings wide the workshop doors.

"Surprise!"

"Ooooh," we gasp. "Ahhhh."

The *Whitefish IV* is big enough for seven people to sit in. It has an air-cooling system, an air-compression system, and an air-purifying system. It has a steam boiler to run the engine and a battery to run the headlights. It has velvet carpeting and comfortable chairs. Along its length are a dozen portholes.

Papa grins. "Who wants to go for a ride?"

"I do!" I whoop.

"Me, too!" says Cyril.

"Don't forget me!" adds Mary.

"Go bye-bye!" squeals the baby.

"Woof!" barks Rex.

"I'm so glad I brought along lunch," says Mama.

One by one we drop down through the hatch.
Then Papa seals it behind us, takes his place at the controls, and . . .

Sploosh!

Swoosh!

Clacketa-clacketa-clacketa!

"WOW!"

Hours later, we rise to the surface.

We glide to the beach.

We spread out a blanket and feast on ham sandwiches.

"Papa," I say between mouthfuls, "that idea was absolutely, positively fantastic!"

"Brilliant," says Cyril.

"Clever," adds Mary.

"Yeaaaa!" squeals the baby.

"Woof!" barks Rex.

"I'm so glad you brought me along," says Mama. She gives Papa a big, big . . .

SMOOOOOCH!

Then a seagull flies overhead.

I toss it my bread crust. "Have you ever wondered what it's like to be a bird?" I ask.

"A bird?" Papa mutters. "A bird?"

"Uh-oh!" squeals the baby.

Clink! Clankety-bang! Thump-whirrrr!

IT'S *ALMOST* TRUE

The *Fool Killer* submarine being raised from the Chicago River in 1915. *Chicago Daily News* negatives collection, DN-0065729. Courtesy of Chicago History Museum.

While this story is fiction, it is based on true events. In the summer of 1851, an eccentric inventor named Lodner Phillips really did take his wife and their children for an afternoon excursion beneath the waves of Lake Michigan. No one knows why Phillips became so obsessed with building a submarine, but for years he worked at making his dream come true. His first attempt was nothing more than a wooden hull that moved by simply pushing a pole along the lake's bottom. It sunk. But Phillips kept trying, and in 1851 he built the *Whitefish*. While it was not the first modern submarine, Phillips did make many important improvements in its design. His innovations included a steering system that allowed the submarine to go left and right rather than just forward and backward, an air-purifying system that kept air fresh for ten hours when up to four people were in the sub, and a boiler that generated steam underwater to run the engine.

Phillips patented his new and improved submarine in 1852, then offered it to the United States Navy. But the Navy wasn't interested. They claimed they wanted only boats that rode on top of the water.

Phillips went on to patent other underwater inventions—"diving armor" for bringing up treasure from shipwrecks, an underwater cannon that could be attached to the outside of a submarine during wartime, and even a machine for making plastic buttons (not all his inventions had to do with submarines). Sadly, before his inventions could bring him either fame or fortune, he died in 1869 when he was just forty-three years old.

As for the submarines he built, all were lost to history until 1915. That year, wreckers digging in the Chicago River (which runs into Lake Michigan) made a startling discovery. A submarine lay half buried in the river's muddy bottom. When it was raised, many people, including members of the Phillips family, claimed it had been built by the inventor just before his death. Placed on daily display in a Chicago storefront, the *Fool Killer*—as people nicknamed it—could be seen for just ten cents. Eventually, the submarine was sold to Parker's Greatest Shows, a traveling carnival that exhibited it across the Midwest. But what happened to the submarine next is anyone's guess. It simply slipped from history and was never seen again.

SOURCES

Little has been written about Lodner Phillips and his inventions. To piece together the major events of his life, I turned to the dedicated local historians at the Michigan City Historical Society in Indiana, as well as a handful of original documents housed in the society's Old Lighthouse Museum. I also tracked down copies of Phillips's patents housed at the National Archives in Washington, D.C., searched for old photographs, and read newspapers, magazines, and scientific lectures of the day. The most helpful sources were these:

Certificate of Death No. 45246—Lodner D. Phillips. Municipal Archives, New York, N.Y.

Gruse Harris, Patricia A. *Great Lakes' First Submarine: L. D. Phillips' "Fool Killer."* Defiance, Ohio: The Hubbard Company, printed for the Michigan City Historical Society, Inc., 1982.

Pesce, G. L. *La Navigation Sous-Marine.* Paris: Librairie de Sciences Générales, 1897.

Pesce, G. L. *La Navigation Sous-Marine.* Paris: Vuibert & Nony, 1906.

Phillips, Lodner D. Steering submarine vessels. US Patent 9,389, filed [unknown], and issued November 9, 1852.

Phillips, Lodner D. Diving armor. US Patent 15,898, filed [unknown], and issued October 14, 1856.

Phillips, Lodner D. Machine for making buttons from plastic materials. US Patent 60,053, filed [unknown], and issued November 27, 1866.

Ragan, Mark K. *Union and Confederate Submarine Warfare in the Civil War.* Cambridge, Mass.: Da Capo Press, 1999.

"Submarine—'Fool Killer'—Now on Exhibition at 208 South State Street." Announcement in the *Chicago Daily Tribune*, February 23, 1916.

For verification of Phillips's family trip beneath the waves of Lake Michigan, as well as for a description of that submarine and its innovations, including an air-purifying system that kept air fresh for ten hours and a steam boiler for generating steam underwater, see:

Barber, F. M. *Lecture on Submarine Boats and Their Application to Torpedo Operations.* Newport, R.I.: U.S. Torpedo Station, 1875.

For additional information regarding the underwater trip, see:

Corbin, Thomas W. *The Romance of Submarine Engineering.* Philadelphia: J. B. Lippincott Company, 1913.